Zebras

Victoria Blakemore

© 2017 Victoria Blakemore

All rights reserved. This book or parts thereof may not be reproduced in any form, stored in any retrieval system, or transmitted in any form by any means—electronic, mechanical, photocopy, recording, or otherwise—without prior written permission of the publisher, except as provided by United States of America copyright law. For permission requests, write to the publisher, at "Attention: Permissions Coordinator," at the address below.

vblakemore.author@gmail.com

Copyright info/picture credits

Cover, Jurgen Vogt/Shutterstock; Page 3, nike159/Pixabay; Page 5, ronbd/Pixabay; Page 7, bosmanerwin/Pixabay; Page 9, ronbd/Pixabay; Pages 10-11, MonikaP/Pixabay; Page 13, Bluesnap/Pixabay; Page 15, igbwebdev/Pixabay; Page 17, Bluesnap/Pixabay; Page 19, UGVERTRIEB/Pixabay; Page 21, Beesmurf/Pixabay; Page 23; kaulvimal/Pixabay; Page 25, scooterenglasias/Pixabay; Page 27, Markjohnson1234/Pixabay; Page 29, AgnethaA/Pixabay; Page 31, nike159/Pixabay; Page 33, Jurgen Vogt/Shutterstock

Table of Contents

What are Zebras?	2
Size	4
Physical Characteristics	6
Habitat	8
Range	10
Diet	12
Communication	16
Movement	18
Zebra Foals	20
Zebra Life	22
Predators	24
Population	26
Zebras in Danger	28
Helping Zebras	30
Glossary	34

What Are Zebras?

Zebras are large mammals. They are related to horses and donkeys.

There are three different kinds of zebras. They differ in where they live and the patterns of their stripes.

Zebras are known for their black and white fur and stripes.

Size

Zebras range in size from about three feet tall to just under six feet tall. The Grevy's zebra is the largest kind of zebra.

Adult zebras can weigh between 440 and 1000 pounds. Most weigh less than 800 pounds.

Male zebras are often larger than female zebras.

Physical Characteristics

Zebras have black and white fur. Some say they are white with black stripes because their belly is white. Actually, their skin is black, so they could also be called black with white stripes.

Every zebra has a different stripe pattern. No two zebras are exactly alike.

Zebras have long eyelashes.

Their eyelashes can help to keep dirt out of their eyes.

Habitat

Most zebras are found in the savannas and grasslands. Some are also found in the mountains.

They need places with lots of grasses to eat and to keep them safe from predators. They also need areas with plenty of water to drink.

Range

Zebras are only found in parts of eastern and southern Africa.

10

They are often seen in Zambia, South Africa, Namibia, Kenya, and Tanzania.

Diet

Zebras are **herbivores**, which means that they eat only plants.

The main food that they eat is grass. They also sometimes eat shrubs, herbs, twigs, leaves, and bark.

Zebras spend a lot of their time **grazing**. They often graze together in groups.

Zebras have very strong, rough teeth. They use them to tear plants when they are eating. They also use their hooves to dig up parts of plants to eat.

They use their back teeth to grind their food down. Their teeth don't get worn down because they never stop growing.

During the dry season, zebras may travel many miles to find water.

Communication

Zebras use mainly sound and movement to communicate with each other.

They move their ears, open their eyes wide, and show their teeth to communicate with each other. A zebra that has it's ears flattened backwards may be angry.

Zebras can bray, snort, puff, and make a barking sound. Some sounds are used as warnings.

Movement

Zebras can run at speeds of up to thirty-five miles per hour. This helps them to outrun some of their predators.

They have very hard hooves. They are able to run over rocky ground without hurting themselves.

If predators are near, mothers and foals often run away. The rest of the zebras may stay and **defend** themselves.

Zebra Foals

Zebras usually have one baby, or foal. When they are born, foals are brown with white stripes. Their color will change as they get older.

Foals are able to walk about twenty minutes after they are born. They can run after about an hour.

Foals **recognize** their mother by their stripes and scent.

Zebra Life

Zebras are social animals. They prefer to spend their time in groups that are called harems or herds.

Zebras sleep standing up. They only sleep when they are in groups, so that some can watch for predators while the others sleep.

Zebras that are in a herd may **groom** each other. They can bite at each other's fur to keep it free from pests.

Predators

Zebras have many different predators. Animals such as lions, hyenas, cheetahs, and leopards hunt zebras.

Groups of zebras work together to defend against predators. They line up in a **semicircle** and kick and bite to protect themselves.

One way zebras stay safe from predators is by using their stripes as **camouflage**.

Population

Some kinds of zebras are **endangered**. There are not many left in the wild. Some could soon become **extinct** if populations continue to **decline**.

The plains zebra, or common zebra, is near threatened. It is not **endangered**.

In the wild, zebras can live as long as thirty-five years.

Zebras in Danger

Zebras are facing many threats. Habitat loss, **poaching**, and disease are some of the main threats.

In some places, zebras are hunted for their meat, bones, and skin. Many times, they are hunted illegally by **poachers**.

Zebra habitats are being destroyed for farmland, buildings, and roads.

Helping Zebras

Many people are trying to help zebra populations.

Special protected areas have been set up to provide animals like zebras with safe habitats. Many places also have wildlife **corridors** that allow animals to travel from one protected area to another.

In many places, hunting zebras is **illegal**. Many governments are trying to keep zebras safe from **poachers**.

Scientists are studying different zebra populations. They hope that learning more about them will help us to protect them.

Glossary

Camouflage: using color to blend in to the surroundings

Corridor: a hall or passageway

Declining: getting smaller

Defend: to protect from harm

Endangered: at risk of becoming extinct

Extinct: when there are no more of an animal left in the wild

Grazing: feeding on growing grass

Groom: to make clean and neat

Herbivore: an animal that eats only plants

Illegal: against the law

Poacher: someone who hunts animals illegally

Poaching: hunting animals illegally

Recognize: to know who someone is

Semicircle: half of a circle

About the Author

Victoria Blakemore is a first grade teacher in Southwest Florida with a passion for reading. You can visit her at www.elementaryexplorers.com

Also in This Series

Also in This Series

Aardvarks	Mako Sharks	Alligators	Frogs	Hedgehogs	Brown Bears	Bongos
Sea Turtles	Quokkas	Muskrats	Zebras	Red Foxes	Ring-Tailed Lemurs	Platypuses
Anteaters	Kangaroos	Rhinos	Jaguars	Wombats	Capybaras	Gorillas
Cats	Skunks	Butterflies	Dingoes	Snow Leopards	African Wild Dogs	Penguins
Whale Sharks	Wolverines	Warthogs	Caracals	Badgers	Seals	Hummingbirds
Pikas	Humpback Whales	Pumas	Lemonade	Llamas	Tulips	Ostriches
Sunflowers	Fennec Foxes

www.ingramcontent.com/pod-product-compliance
Lightning Source LLC
Chambersburg PA
CBHW040221040426
42333CB00049B/3211